NATIONAL GEOGRAPHIC

EXPLORE OUR WORLD

STUDENT BOOK **2**

SERIES EDITORS
JoAnn (Jodi) Crandall   Joan Kang Sh

AUTHORS
Gabrielle Pritchard
Diane Pinkley

NATIONAL GEOGRAPHIC LEARNING | CENGAGE Learning

Australia • Brazil • Japan • Korea • Mexico • Singapore • Spain • United Kingdom • United States

Unit 0
My Family

sister

mom

dad

grandpa

grandma

me

1 **Look, listen, and repeat.** TR: 2

2 **Listen.** Point and say. TR: 3

2

aunt

cousin

uncle

3 **Work with a partner.** Point. Ask and answer.

Who's that?

It's his cousin!

At School

Work in a group.

Raise your hand.

Be quiet!

Hold up your card.

4 **Look, listen, and repeat.** TR: 4

5 **Listen, point, and say.** TR: 5

Close your book.

Go to the board.

Open your book.

Take out your crayons.

Work with a partner.

6 **Work in a group.** Say and do.
Take turns.

Open your books.

5

7 Listen, point, and say. TR: 6

I

You

He

She

It

We

You

They

8 Read and look. Write the number.

1. He's in the kitchen.
2. It's big.
3. You're strong.
4. She's reading.

5. I'm tall.
6. They're my parents.
7. We're friends.
8. You're young.

9 Listen and say. TR: 7

This is **my** teddy bear.

Is this **your** pencil?

It's **his** bike.

Her sandwich looks good.

Its name is Jay-jay.

This is **our** kite.

That's **your** ball.

It's **their** puzzle.

6

Numbers

0
zero

1
one

2
two

3
three

4
four

5
five

6
six

7
seven

8
eight

9
nine

10
ten

11
eleven

12
twelve

13
thirteen

14
fourteen

15
fifteen

16
sixteen

17
seventeen

18
eighteen

19
nineteen

20
twenty

10 **Listen, point, and repeat.** TR: 8

11 **Work with a partner.** Point and say.

Animal Friends

Look and check.

The bird is white.

 yes   ○ no

The monkey likes the bird.

○ yes   ○ no

Macaque monkey and dove,
Neilingding Island, China

1 **Listen and say.** TR: 9

2 **Listen.** Point and say. TR: 10

a dog

a turtle

a cat

10

a horse

a goat

a chicken

a sheep

a duck

a cow

3 **Work with a partner.**
Point. Ask and answer.

What is it?

It's a turtle.

GRAMMAR TR: 11

What **are** the horses **doing?**	They**'re running.**
Are the sheep **sleeping?**	No, they **aren't.**
Are they **eating?**	Yes, they **are.**

4 **Listen and find.** Write. TR: 12

1. ___They're running.___   2. _____

3. _____   4. _____

5 Listen and say. TR: 13

see

climb

fly

swim

crawl

6 Work with a partner. Point and say.

7 Look. Listen and read. (Circle) *yes* or *no.* TR: 14

1. The birds are flying.   yes   no
2. The cat is swimming.   yes   no
3. The turtle is crawling.   yes   no

8 Work with a partner. Say and stick.

Number 1. The dogs are sleeping.

Number 2. The butterfly is flying.

1   2   3   4   5

Do you **want to ride** the goat? No, I don't.
What **do** you **want to do**? I **want to ride** the horse.
What **does** Anna **want to do**? She **wants to see** the ducks.

9 **Look.** Listen and read. Write. TR: 16

What does Maria want to do?

1. Maria _____ the sheep.

Does Carlos want to see the ducks?

2. No, Carlos _____ the frog.

10 **Play a game.** Cut out the cards on page 97.
Ask and answer. Play with a partner.

11 **Listen.** Read and sing. TR: 17

Animals

I see animals.
What are they doing?
I see animals.
Can you see them, too?

THE SOUNDS OF ENGLISH TR: 18

dog

12 **Listen and say.**

1. **d**og   **d**uck

2. **d**esk   **d**oll

3. be**d**room   bir**d**

13 **Listen and read.** TR: 19

Animal Babies

Do you like babies? Do you like animal babies? Let's learn about some animals and their babies. Cats have many baby cats, called kittens. Baby dogs are called puppies. Baby chickens are called chicks. Baby sheep are called lambs. A baby elephant is called a calf.

Baby Asian elephant

14 **Work with a partner.** Ask and answer. What are your favorite animals?

What are your favorite animals?

I like dogs and turtles.

16

**Be good
to animals.**

Give your pet
food and water.

**Are you good to animals?
What do you do?**

NATIONAL
GEOGRAPHIC

A hiker and her dog, the Himalayas

Fun in Class

Look and check.

The boys are

○ walking.

○ jumping.

Sack race, Machiques, Venezuela

1 **Listen and say.** TR: 20

2 **Listen, point, and say.** TR: 21

counting

coloring

talking

cutting

drawing

gluing

erasing

3 **Work with a partner.** Point. Ask and answer.

What are they doing?

They're talking.

21

What **are** you **doing?**   We**'re counting** crayons.

4 **Look.** Listen and number the pictures. TR: 23

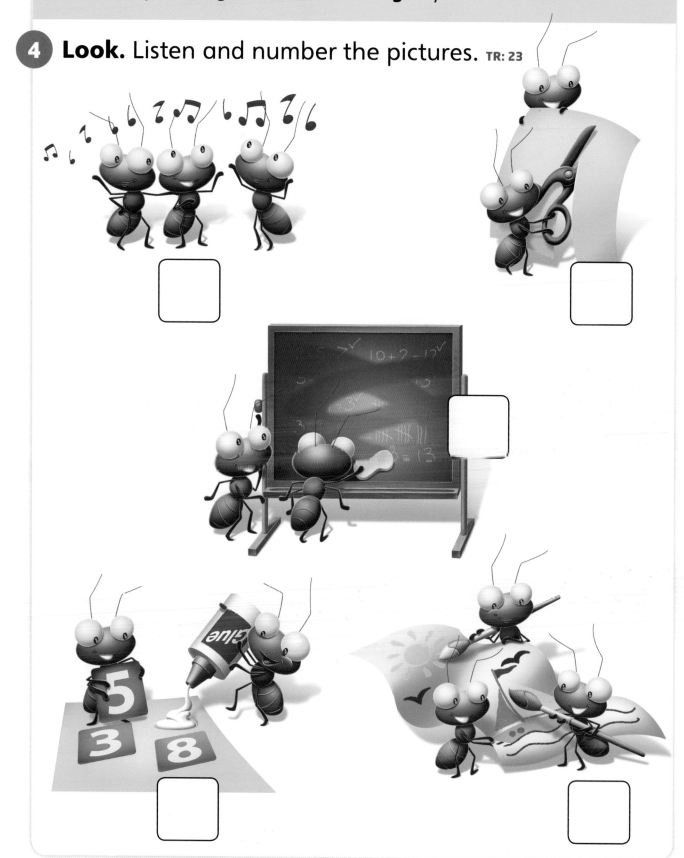

5 **Listen and say.** Read and write. TR: 24

a marker

a notebook

glue

a paintbrush

scissors

1. I'm writing. I'm using ___a notebook___.

2. I'm painting. I'm using _____.

3. I'm drawing. I'm using _____.

4. I'm gluing. I'm using _____.

5. I'm cutting. I'm using _____.

6 **Listen and stick.** TR: 25

1	2	3	4	5

Are there any markers on the desk?   No, there aren't.
Are there any markers in the closet?   Yes, there are.

7 **Read.** Look and write.

1. Are there any red paintbrushes on page 22?

   Yes, there are.

2. Are there any scissors on page 20?

   _____

3. Are there any notebooks on page 23?

   _____

4. Are there any green markers on page 18?

   _____

5. Are there any pencils on page 20?

   _____

8 **Play a game.** Cut out page 99 and color
the pictures. Play with a partner.

Are there any
red crayons?

No, sorry. Now
it's my turn.

9 **Listen.** Read and sing. TR: 27

Our Classroom

Reading, writing, talking, listening.
Counting, gluing, cutting, drawing.

What are you doing today?
What are you doing in your classroom?
What are you doing today?
What are you doing in your classroom?

THE SOUNDS OF ENGLISH TR: 28

counting

10 **Listen and say.**

1. **c**ounting   **c**utting

2. **c**oloring   **c**ooking

3. **c**omputer   so**c**k

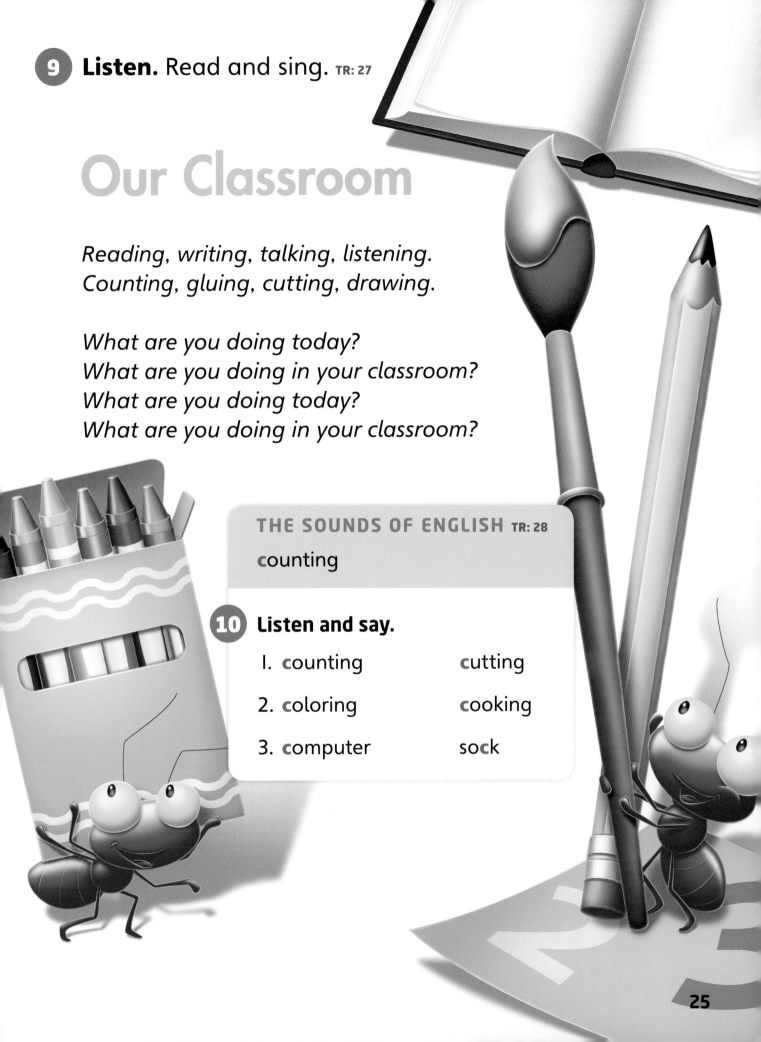

Paper Art

This girl is making Chinese paper art. She is cutting paper to make a picture of a cat. She is using scissors. Some people make paper animals or flowers.

In Mexico people make paper art, too. People cut pictures of flowers, animals, and people.

12 **Work with a partner.** Read. Ask and answer.

1. Do you like to fold and cut paper?

2. What can you make?

Weird but true You can fold a regular piece of paper in half only seven times.

China

Mexico

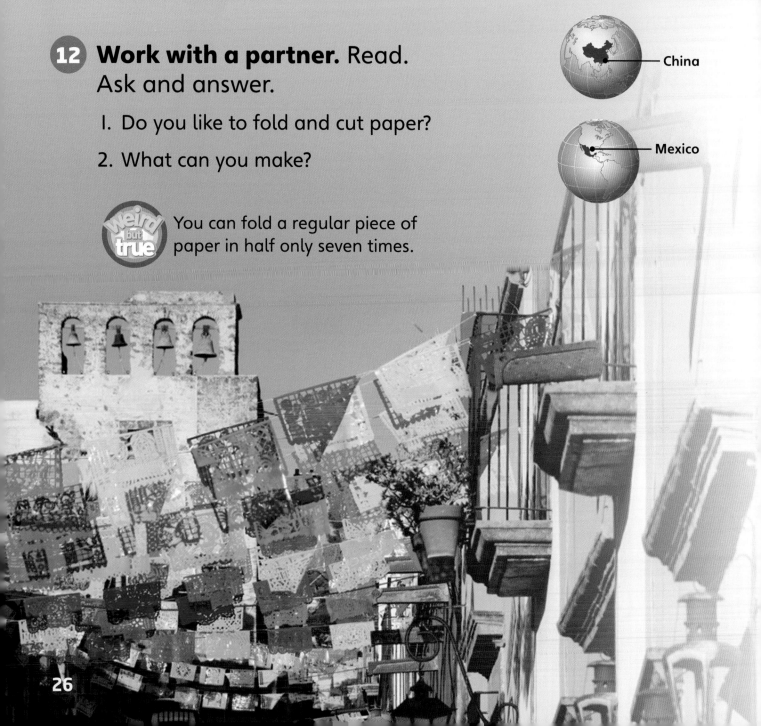

Be neat.

Put away
your things.

Are you neat at school and at home?
What do you do?

NATIONAL GEOGRAPHIC

Classroom, Tokyo, Japan

Boots and Bathing Suits

Look and check.

The girl is wearing a dress.

◯ yes   ◯ no

She is wearing gloves.

◯ yes   ◯ no

Girl making snow angel

a raincoat

cloudy

rainy

boots

30

a bathing suit

hot

sunny

cold

3 **Work with a partner.**
Point and say. Use the words.

pants   boots   gloves
a jacket   a raincoat

It's cloudy and rainy.

She's wearing a raincoat and boots.

What**'s** the weather **like?**   **It's** rainy.

4 **Point and say.** What's the weather like?

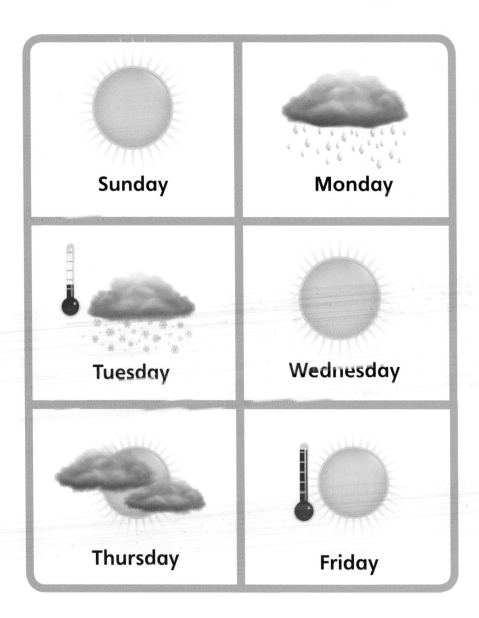

Sunday

Monday

Tuesday

Wednesday

Thursday

Friday

It's cold today.
What day is it?

It's Tuesday.

shorts

an umbrella

sneakers

a coat

jeans

1. They're ___green shorts___ .

2. They're _____ .

3. It's _____ .

4. It's _____ .

5. They're _____ .

6 **Talk and stick.** Take turns.

I wear socks with these.

I know! They're sneakers!

1   2   3   4   5

It's cold. **Put on** your coat.
It's hot. **Take off** your jacket.
It's rainy. **Don't forget** your umbrella.

7 **Read.** Underline the correct answer.

1. It's cloudy. Put on your **dress. / raincoat.**

2. It's rainy. Don't forget your **boots. / jeans.**

3. It's sunny. Take off your **raincoat. / sneakers.**

4. It's cold. Don't forget your **umbrella. / gloves.**

5. It's hot. Put on your **coat. / shorts.**

8 **Play a game.** Cut out the cards on page 101.
Play with a partner.

It's hot.

Put on your bathing suit.

Good. Your turn.

9 **Listen. Read and sing.** TR: 35

Hot or Cold?

We dress for the weather.
The weather can be hot or cold.
Sometimes it's hot. Sometimes it's cold.
Is it hot or cold today?

THE SOUNDS OF ENGLISH TR: 36

rainy

10 **Listen and say.**

1. rainy   raincoat
2. river   rock
3. erasing   car

Boy sledding in Seoul, South Korea

11 **Listen and read.** TR: 37

Snow Animals

The Arctic is a very cold and snowy place. The polar bear, arctic fox, and arctic hare are arctic animals. Their fur keeps them warm. It hides them in the snow. The arctic fox and the arctic hare have white fur in the winter and brown fur in the summer.

 Polar bears are black under their fur.

arctic fox

arctic hare

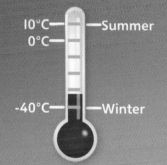

12 **Work with a partner.** Which animals live in cold places?

What about cats?

Cats can live in cold places.

Dress for the weather.

What's the weather like?
Look. Put on the right clothes.

How do you dress for the weather?

Bergueda, Catalonia, Spain

Fun in the Sun

Look and check.

The boys are

◯ walking. ◯ jumping.

They all have

◯ buckets. ◯ shirts.

Boys playing in the water, Klungkung, Bali

jump rope

play a
game

fly a kite

ride a bike

play soccer

play baseball

play basketball

3 **Work with a partner.** Point. Ask and answer.

What are they doing?

They're playing basketball.

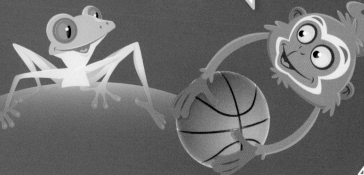

Do you **like to play** baseball?	Yes, I do. It's fun.
Do you **like to jump** rope?	No, I don't. It's boring.
What do you **like to do?**	I **like to play** baseball.
What do they **like to do?**	They **like to swim**.

4 **Work in a group of three. Take turns.**
Ask and answer. Tell the class about your group.

What do you like to do?

I like to play soccer.

42

5 Listen and say. TR: 41

bounce a ball

throw a ball

catch a ball

watch a game

play tag

6 Read. Look at the pictures. Match.

1. I like to bounce a ball. __a__   2. I like to throw a ball. _____

3. They like to catch a ball. _____   4. I like to watch a game. _____

7 Say and stick. Work with a partner.

Do you like to play tag?

No, I don't.

1   2   3   4   5

Let's throw a ball. OK. What fun! 😊

Let's bounce a ball. No, thanks. 😞

8 **Read, write, and draw.** What do you think?

1. <u>Let's play</u> soccer. ⟶ 😞

2. _____ a game. ⟶ ◯

3. _____ a ball. ⟶ ◯

4. _____ tag. ⟶ ◯

5. _____ rope. ⟶ ◯

9 **Play a game.** Cut out the pictures and the cube on page 103. Glue. Play with a partner.

Let's fly a kite!

Ok. What fun!

10 Listen. Read and sing. TR: 43

Outside

What is fun for you?
What do you like to do?
Do you like to play?
Let's play outside all day.

THE SOUNDS OF ENGLISH TR: 44

s**u**n

11 Listen and say.

1. f**u**n   s**u**n
2. j**u**mp   r**u**n
3. b**u**g   d**u**ck

A Big Ball of Fun

These girls are in big balls. The balls are very strong. The girls like to play in the balls. They can walk, jump, or run. They're having fun!

13 **Work with a partner.**
How many kinds of balls can you name?

Hamsters run in balls, too!

15 cm (6 in.)

2 m (6.6 feet)

Be a good sport.

**Play by the rules. Be fair
and take turns. Have fun!**

Are you a good sport?

Review

Start

Sing your favorite song.

GLue

Hop in a circle.

Work in groups. Look and play. Ask and answer.

Do you like to play basketball?

Yes, I do.

Finish

Inside Our House

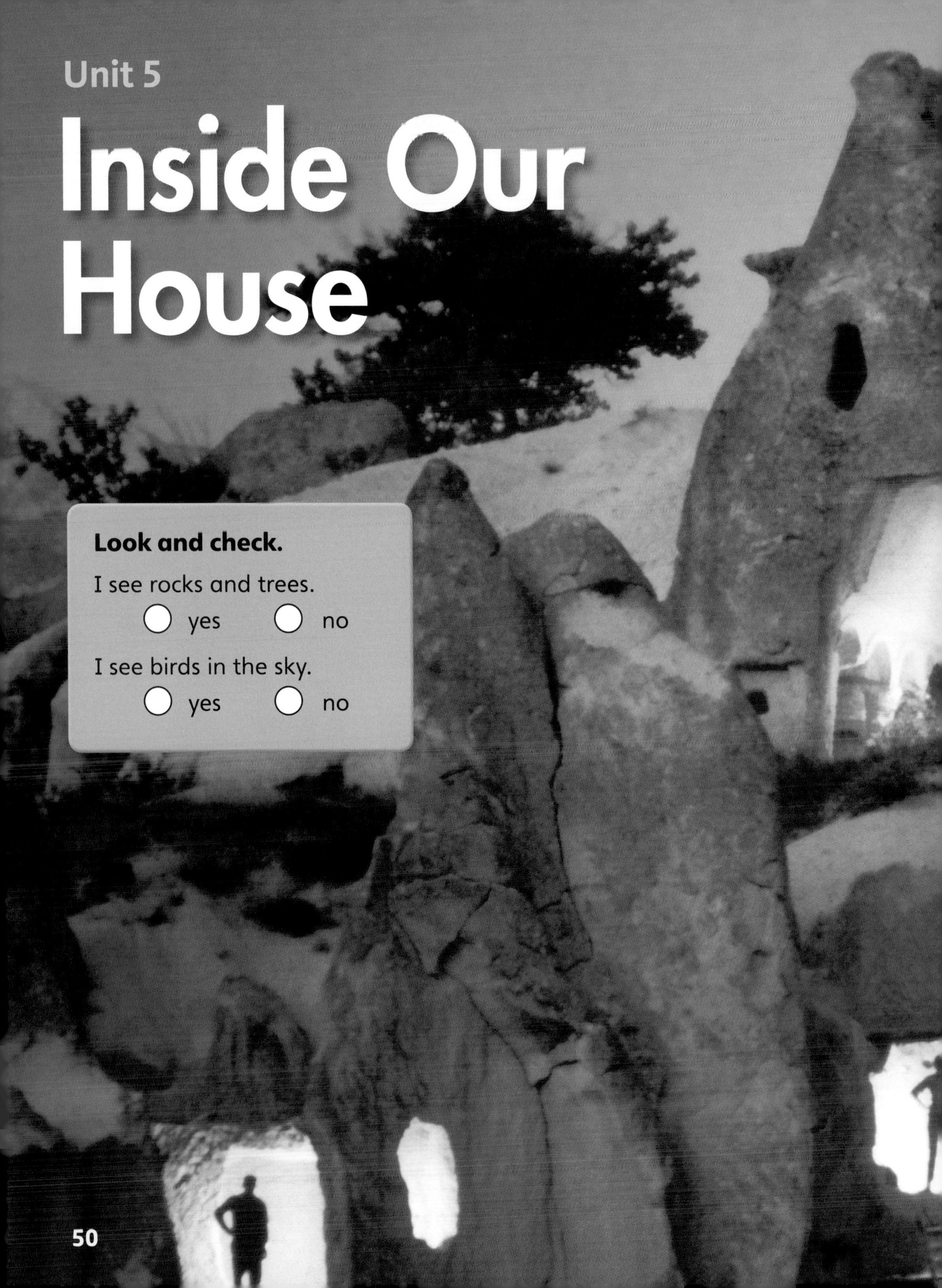

Look and check.

I see rocks and trees.

○ yes ○ no

I see birds in the sky.

○ yes ○ no

Cave house, Cappadocia, Turkey

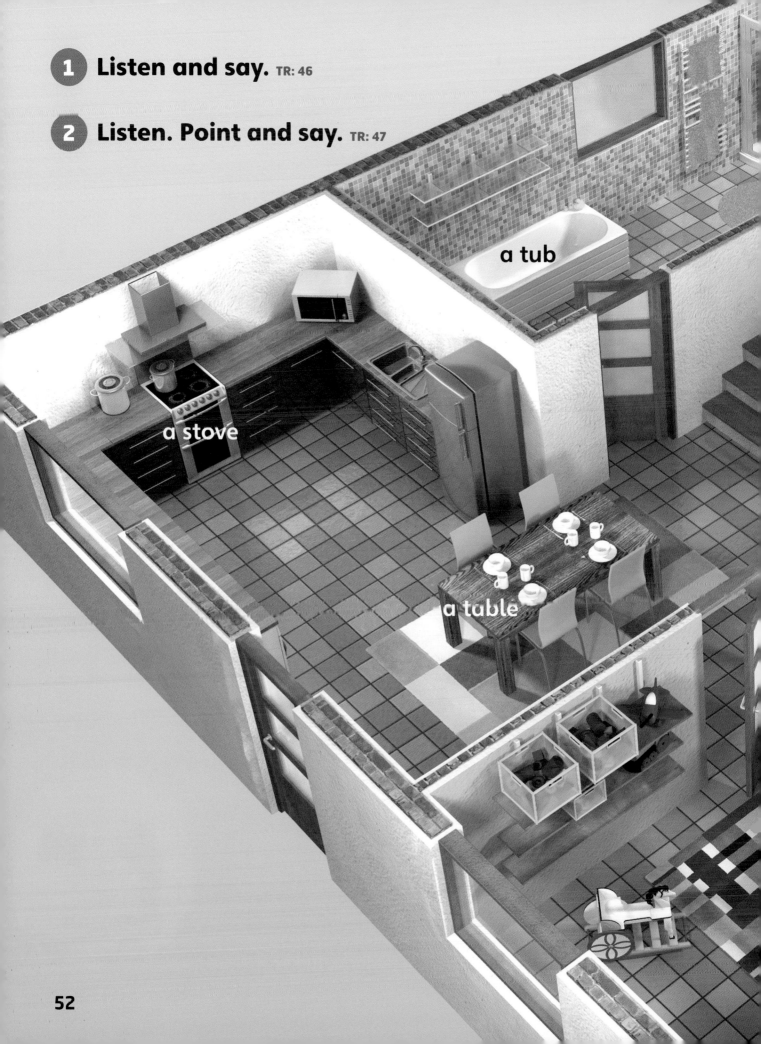

1 **Listen and say.** TR: 46

2 **Listen. Point and say.** TR: 47

a tub

a stove

a table

52

a shower

a bookcase

stairs

a rug

Is there a rug in the living room?

Yes, there is.

53

above

behind

in front of

between

next to

under

4 **Play a game.** Cut out the cards on page 105. Play with a partner.

The frog is in front of the TV.

5 **Listen and say.** Look and write. TR: 49

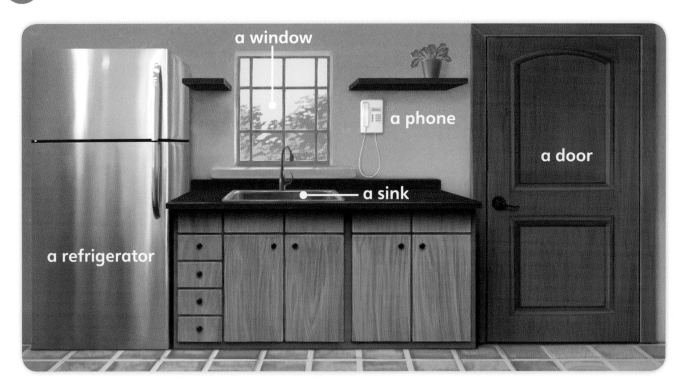

a window

a phone

a door

a sink

a refrigerator

1. There is a small shelf between the _____

   and the _____.

2. There is a _____ under the big shelf.

3. There is a window above the _____.

4. The plant is next to the _____.

6 **Listen and stick.** Compare your answers. TR: 50

Where is the phone?   It's on the shelf.

behind	between	next to	under	on

| Where is the **phone?** | **It**'s in the kitchen. |
| Where are the **lamps?** | **They**'re in the living room. |

7 **Play a game.** Look and remember.
Play with a partner.

Where are
the chairs?

They're in the kitchen. I think
they're in front of the door.

8 **Look at the picture.** Write about the cat,
frogs, flowers, and umbrella.

My House

Welcome to my house.
This is where I live.
Welcome to my living room.
Is there a place to sit?

The armchair is in front of the fireplace.
Sit down and warm your feet.
The fireplace is next to the bookcase.
Let's find a book to read.

THE SOUNDS OF ENGLISH TR: 53

t**a**ble

10 **Listen and say.**

1. t**a**ble   bookc**a**se

2. b**a**seball   g**a**me

3. er**a**ser   cr**a**yon

11 **Listen and read.** TR: 54

Fun Houses

Airplane House

Jo-Ann Ussery's house is an airplane. It has lots of windows. There's a living room, a dining room, a kitchen, and three bedrooms.

airplane house

Egg House

Dai Haifei's house has only one room inside. In the room there's a bed, a small table, and a lamp. There aren't any chairs.

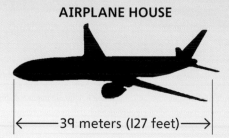

AIRPLANE HOUSE

←— 39 meters (127 feet) —→

EGG HOUSE

3 meters (10 feet)

12 **Work with a partner.** Talk about your house. Take turns.

Weird but true

In this house, everything is upside down!

58

Help at home.

Help your family.
Help with the chores.

How can you help at home?

NATIONAL GEOGRAPHIC

Day by Day

Look and check.

The bird is

○ eating.

○ taking a bath.

The bird is

○ in a bowl.

○ in a tub.

Parrot taking a bath, Costa Rica

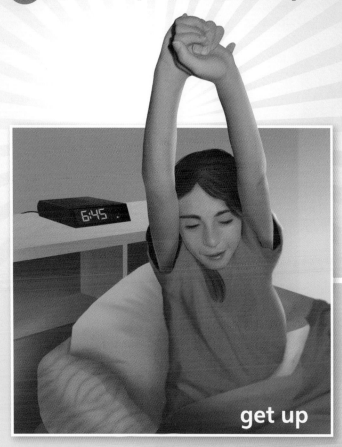

get up

brush
my teeth

go to school

eat lunch

play with
friends

I get up. Then I brush my teeth.

I brush my teeth. Then I get dressed.

get dressed | **eat breakfast**

eat dinner

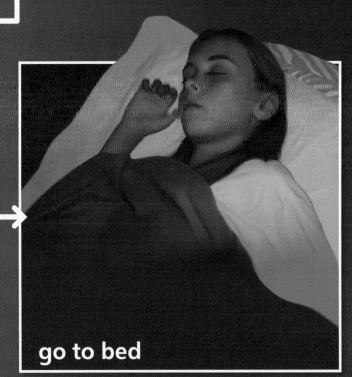

go to bed

What time is it?	**It's** 1:00.	It's one **o'clock.**
When do you get up?	**At** 7:00.	At seven **o'clock.**
When does he go to bed?	**At** 9:00.	At nine **o'clock.**

4 **Play a game.** Cut out the cubes on page 107. Play with a partner. Ask and say.

What time is it?

It's seven o'clock.

When does he wash his face?

At seven o'clock.

5 **Listen and say.** Listen. Read and underline. TR: 58

in the morning

in the afternoon

in the evening

at night

1. Hana plays baseball in the **morning / afternoon.**

2. She watches TV **in the evening / at night.**

3. Berto rides his bike in the **evening / morning.**

4. He plays games **at night / in the afternoon.**

6 **Work with a partner.** Say and stick.

When do you play with friends?

In the afternoon.

morning	afternoon	evening	night

What do you do **every day?**   I **always** play with my sister.

What does your brother do on Saturday?
He sleeps! He **never** gets up before 10:00.

I ride my bike to school every morning.

7 **Play a game.** Play with a partner. Say.

8 **Write.** Work in groups of four. Talk about your partner.

My partner always _____.

_____ never _____.

_____ every day.

9 **Listen. Read and sing.** TR: 60

Day by Day

What time is it? What time is it?
What time is it? Can you tell me?

It's seven o'clock. It's seven o'clock.
It's seven o'clock in the morning.
I always get up at seven o'clock.
I get up at seven every day.

THE SOUNDS OF ENGLISH TR: 61

go

10 **Listen and say.**

1. **g**o   **g**et up

2. **g**ame   le**g**

3. bi**g**   do**g**

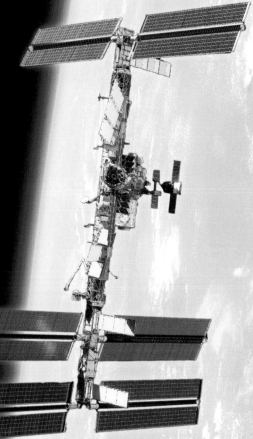

A Day in the Space Station

Astronauts at the International Space Station are busy all day. They get up at seven o'clock. Then they eat breakfast. At eight o'clock they start experiments.

At one o'clock the astronauts eat lunch. In the afternoon they do more experiments. Sometimes they spacewalk outside.

At seven o'clock they eat dinner. In the evening the astronauts read or send e-mails. At about ten o'clock they go to bed.

eat lunch

go to bed

90 minutes

Astronauts grow about 5 cm (2 in.) in space.

12 **Work with a partner.** Talk about your day. How is it different from an astronaut's day? How is it the same?

The astronauts get up at seven o'clock.

I get up at seven o'clock, too. What about you?

Be on time.

Don't be late.
Plan your day.

How can you be on time?

NATIONAL GEOGRAPHIC

Subway, Tokyo, Japan

How Are You?

Look and check.

The big girl is happy.

◯ yes   ◯ no

She's wearing a red dress.

◯ yes   ◯ no

Sanaa, Yemen

1 **Listen and say.** TR: 63

2 **Listen. Point and say.** TR: 64

scared

tired

angry

3 **Work with a partner.** Ask and answer.

Is he hungry?

No. He's thirsty.

hungry

thirsty

bored

surprised

How are you?   I'm OK.   I'm fine.   I'm great!

He **looks** bored.   No. He's tired.
She **looks** happy.   Yes. It's her birthday.

4 **Listen.** Write the number. Draw. TR: 66

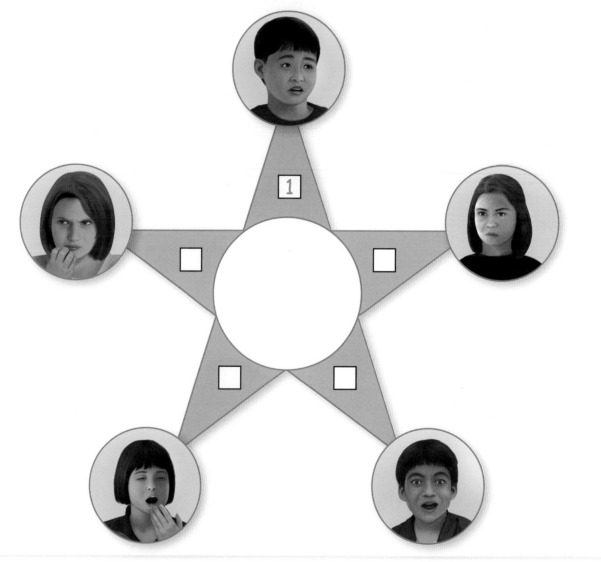

He looks scared.

No. He's surprised.

5 **Listen and say.** Circle the letter. TR: 67

laughing

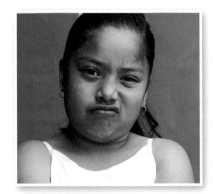
frowning

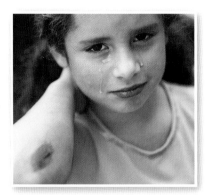
crying

smiling

yawning

1. My cat is   a. yawning.   b. frowning.

2. The boy is   a. laughing.   b. smiling.

3. The girl is   a. crying.   b. yawning.

4. My sister is   a. smiling.   b. laughing.

5. The girl is   a. frowning.   b. crying.

6 **Work with a partner.** Talk. Guess and stick.

This is a girl.

Is she smiling?

Yes. It's your turn.

1   2   3   4   5

parent	**parents**	Our **parents** are taking us to the circus.
person	**people**	Some **people** don't like the circus.
child	**children**	Most **children** like the circus.

7 **Read and write.**

1. The _____ are smiling at the teacher. (student)

2. The _____ are laughing at the puppet. (child)

3. Some _____ are worried about the time. (person)

4. My _____ are angry about my messy room. (parent)

5. Most _____ and _____ like sports. (boy/girl)

8 **Play a game.** Cut out the cards on page 109. Play with a partner.

These children are sad.

That's right. My turn.

9 **Listen. Read and sing.** TR: 69

Emotions

How are you?
How do you feel?
How are you?
Tell me, please. How do you feel?

It's OK to be happy,
or sometimes to feel sad.
It's OK to be silly,
or sometimes to feel mad.

THE SOUNDS OF ENGLISH TR: 70

tired

10 **Listen and say.**

1. tired   surprised

2. night   kite

3. bike   rice

Fabulous Faces

People from all over the world paint their faces. This Native American girl paints her face to show she's proud of her community and traditions.

— North America

Others paint their faces to make people feel scared. The man from India has a scary, green face.

People paint their faces for fun, too. When some fans go to watch sports, they paint their faces.

In some places, people paint children's faces at parties. The children like to have pictures of flowers or animals on their faces.

12 **Work with a partner.** Talk about face painting.

What do you want on your face?

I want a butterfly.

weird but true

People can make more than 10,000 different expressions with their faces.

— India

Be kind.

Help your friends and family.
Be kind to other people.

Are you kind? What do you do?

Awesome Animals

Look and check.

This animal is a

○ bird.   ○ frog.

This animal can

○ jump.   ○ fly.

Red-eyed tree frog, Central America

1 **Listen and say.** TR: 72

2 **Listen. Point and say.** TR: 73

a tiger

a lion

a zebra

a giraffe

a panda

a penguin

a hippo

a kangaroo

swing

hop

3 **Work with a partner.** Ask and answer. Use these words.

| climb | fly | hop | jump |
| run | swim | swing | walk |

This animal can hop. What is it?

It's a kangaroo!

Can a penguin swim?	Yes, it **can**. A penguin **can** swim.
Can penguins fly?	No, they **can't**. Penguins **can't** fly.

4 **Play a game.** Play with a partner.

Can a lion jump?

Yes, it can.

84

5 **Listen and say.** Check T for *True* and F for *False*. TR: 75

colorful feathers

sharp claws

a short tail

a long trunk

big teeth

1. Kangaroos have colorful feathers.   T   F
2. Elephants have long trunks.   T   F
3. Pandas have sharp claws.   T   F
4. Monkeys have short tails.   T   F
5. Lions have sharp teeth.   T   F

6 **Work with a partner.** Talk and stick.

Do hippos have long legs?

No, they have short legs.

short legs	long tails	sharp claws	long necks	big ears

Does a tiger **have** sharp claws?　　Yes, it **does.**
Does a tiger **have** a trunk?　　No, it **doesn't.**

Do tigers **have** sharp claws?　　Yes, they **do.**
Do tigers **have** trunks?　　No, they **don't.**

7 **Read and check.** Then listen and compare your answers. TR: 77

	big ears	long neck	sharp teeth	long trunk	colorful feathers
elephant	✓				
giraffe					
lion					
parrot					

8 **Play a game.** Cut out the cards on page 111. Play with a partner.

Do giraffes have short necks?

No, they don't. They have long necks.

Awesome Animals

I want to be a monkey in a tree!
And I want to fly high up in the sky!
I want to be a monkey in a tree!
And I want to fly high up in the sky!

THE SOUNDS OF ENGLISH TR: 79

ze**bra**

10   Listen and say.

1. **z**ebra   **sh**eep

2. **t**ee**th**   **tr**ee

3. **j**ean**s**   **t**ea

Two Big Birds

Cassowary

The cassowary is big and strong. It can live to be 60 years old. It lives in Papua New Guinea and Australia.

The cassowary can run really fast, but it can't fly. Watch out! An angry cassowary can kick really hard!

Ostrich

The ostrich is big and strong. It can live to be 50 years old. It lives in Africa.

Like the cassowary, the ostrich can run really fast, but it can't fly. And yes, it can kick hard, too!

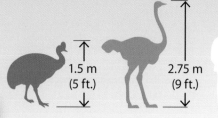

1.5 m (5 ft.)   2.75 m (9 ft.)

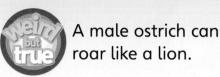 A male ostrich can roar like a lion.

12 **Work with a partner.** Talk about the animals.

giraffes   kangaroos   tigers   zebras

Zebras live in Africa.

Respect animals.

It's important to
respect animals.
Be kind and gentle.

How can we respect animals?

NATIONAL
GEOGRAPHIC

Jane Goodall
with chimpanzees

Miss a turn.

Start

Finish

90

Go back one space.

Work with a partner.
Spin. Ask and answer.

When do you get up?

At 7 o'clock.

91

NATIONAL GEOGRAPHIC
EXPLORE OUR WORLD

TR: 81

This is our world.
Everybody's got a song to sing.
Each boy and girl.
This is our world!

I say "our!" You say "world!"
Our!
World!
Our!
World!

I say "boy!" You say "girl!"
Boy!
Girl!
Boy!
Girl!

I say "Everybody move…"
I say "Everybody stop…"
Everybody stop!

This is our world.
Everybody's got a song to sing.
Each boy and girl.
This is our world!

Let's sing!

Unit 1 Animals TR: 17

I see animals.
What are they doing?
I see animals.
Can you see them, too?

What do you see?

I see one dog.
Is it running?
Yes, it's running.
It's running in the sun.

What do you see?

I see two cats.
Are they climbing?
Yes, they're climbing.
They're climbing, and it's fun.

Running and climbing,
hopping and singing.
These are things we like to
    do.

Are you ready?
All together!
Run! Climb! Hop! Sing!

What do you see?

I see three frogs.
Are they hopping?
Yes, they're hopping.
They're hopping on a rock.

What do you see?

I see four birds.
Are they singing?
Yes, they're singing.
They're singing la, la, la!

La lalala!
La lala!

Running and climbing,
hopping and singing.
These are things we like
    to do.

Are you ready?
All together!
Run! Climb! Hop! Sing!

Unit 2 Our Classroom TR: 27

Reading, writing, talking, listening.
Counting, gluing, cutting, drawing.

What are you doing today?
What are you doing in your classroom?
What are you doing today?
What are you doing in your classroom?

We're cutting. We're gluing.
We're coloring pictures.
We're cutting. We're gluing.
We're coloring pictures.

CHORUS

We're talking. We're writing.
We're listening to our teacher.
We're talking. We're writing.
We're listening to a story.

Reading, writing, talking, listening.

Counting, gluing, cutting, drawing.
Reading, writing, talking, listening.
Counting, gluing, cutting, drawing.
Reading, writing, talking, listening.
Counting, gluing, cutting, drawing.
We're having fun!

What are you doing today?
What are you doing in your classroom?
What are you doing today?
What are you doing in your classroom?

Unit 3 Hot or Cold? TR: 35

Come and look outside.
What do you see?
Today it's snowy.
Put on your boots and coat.
It's cold outside today.

Come and look outside.
What do you see?
Today it's sunny. Put on
    your sneakers and shorts.
It's hot outside today.

We dress for the weather.
The weather can be hot or cold.
Sometimes it's hot, sometimes it's cold.
Is it hot or cold today?

Take off your boots and your sweater.
Take off your hat and your coat.
What's the weather like?
Is it hot? Yes!
It's hot outside today.

Put on your boots and your sweater.
Put on your hat and your coat.
What's the weather like?
Is it cold? Yes!
It's cold outside today.

CHORUS

Unit 4 Outside TR: 43

Hey! What do you like to
    do outside?

I like to ride a bike.
Yes, I do. Yes, I do.
I like to fly a kite.
Yes, I do. Yes, I do.
I like to play games.
I like to play outside
    with you.
It's fun, fun, fun!

What is fun for you?
What do you like to do?
Do you like to play?
Let's play outside all day.

What is fun for you?
What do you like to do?
Do you like to play?
Let's play outside all day.
What is fun for you?

Do you like to skateboard?
No, I don't.
Play hide and seek?
No, I don't.
Play basketball?
No. It's boring.

CHORUS

I like to jump rope.
Yes, I do. Yes, I do.
I like to rollerblade.
Yes, I do. Yes, I do.
I like to play soccer.
I like to play with you.
It's fun, fun, fun!

CHORUS

Unit 5 **My House** TR: 52

Welcome to my house.
This is where I live.
Welcome to my living room.
Is there a place to sit?

The armchair is in front of
the fireplace.
Sit down and warm your
feet.
The fireplace is next to the
bookcase.
Let's find a book to read.

Welcome to my house.
This is where I live.
Welcome to my kitchen.
Is there food in there?

The refrigerator is between
the windows.
There's lots of food inside.
Something's cooking on the
stove.
May I try some? May I,
please?

Welcome to my house.
This is where I live.
Welcome to my bedroom.
Is there a place to sleep?

My pillow is on my bed.
It's where I put my head.
I turn off the light above
me.
And then I go to sleep.

Where is the fireplace? It's in
the living room.
Where is the stove? It's in
the kitchen.
Where is the light? It's in the
bedroom.

Welcome to my house.
This is where I live.
It was nice to see you.
Please come again!
Welcome to my house!

Unit 6 **Day by Day** TR: 60

What time is it?
What time is it?
What time is it?
Can you tell me?

It's seven o'clock. It's seven o'clock.
It's seven o'clock in the morning.
I always get up at seven o'clock.
I get up at seven every day.

CHORUS

It's eight o'clock. It's eight o'clock.
It's eight o'clock in the morning.
I go to school at eight o'clock.
I always go to school at eight.

CHORUS

It's three o'clock. It's three o'clock.
It's three o'clock in the afternoon.
I always play with friends at three o'clock.
I play with my friends every day.

CHORUS

It's nine o'clock. It's nine o'clock.
It's nine o'clock at night.
I go to sleep at nine o'clock.
I go to sleep at nine every day.

Unit 7 Emotions TR: 69

Sometimes I'm happy.
Sometimes I'm surprised.
Sometimes I'm just silly.
I'm laughing inside!

Sometimes I'm angry.
Sometimes I'm just bored.
Sometimes I'm excited.

How are you?
How do you feel?
How are you?
Tell me, please. How do you feel?

Sometimes I'm smiling.
I'm laughing at a joke!
Sometimes I'm crying.
I feel sad.

Sometimes I'm tired.
Sometimes I'm worried.
Sometimes I'm feeling scared.

It's OK to be happy,
or sometimes to feel sad.
It's OK to be silly,
or sometimes to feel mad.

CHORUS

CHORUS

Unit 8 Awesome Animals TR: 78

A parrot is a bird that flies.
It can't swim, but it can fly.
A parrot is a bird that flies
   high in the sky.

A monkey swings from tree to tree,
tree to tree, tree to tree.
A monkey swings from tree to tree.
Why can't we?

I want to be a monkey in a tree!
I want to fly high up in the sky!

A penguin is a bird that swims.
It can't fly, but it can swim.
A penguin is a bird that swims
   deep in the sea.

A kangaroo can hop and jump.
It can't climb, but it can jump.
A kangaroo can hop and jump
   just like me.

I want to be a monkey in a tree!
And I want to fly high up in the sky!
I want to be a monkey in a tree!
And I want to fly high up in the sky!

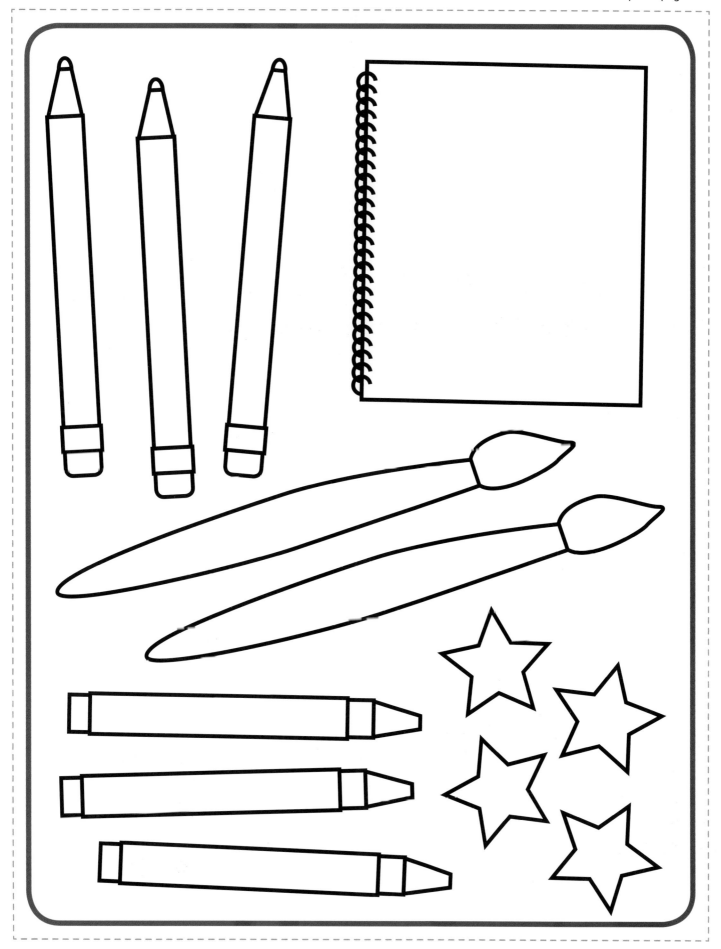

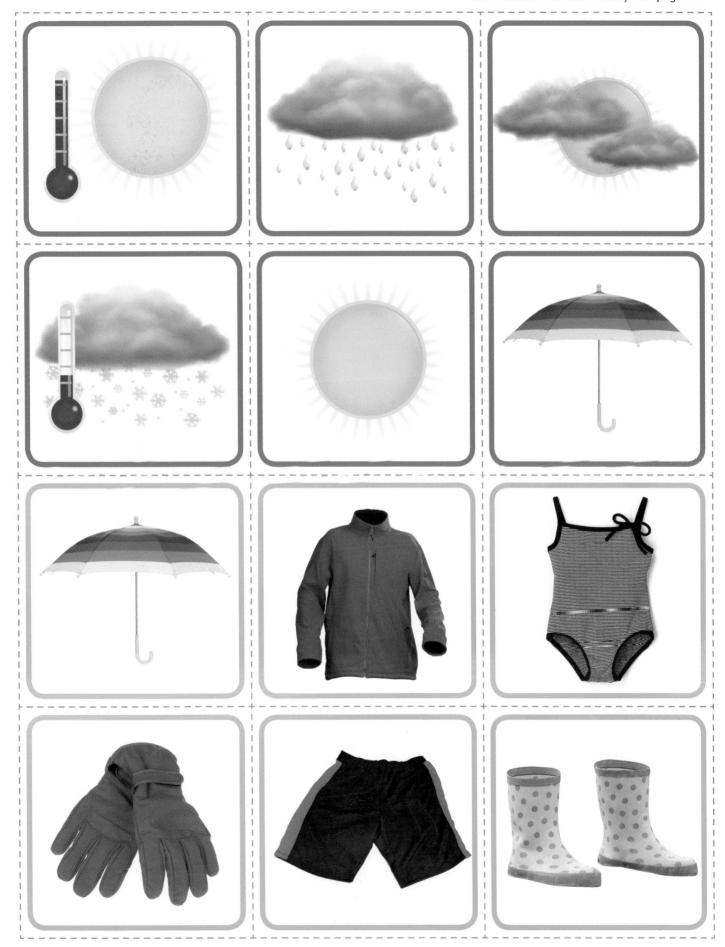

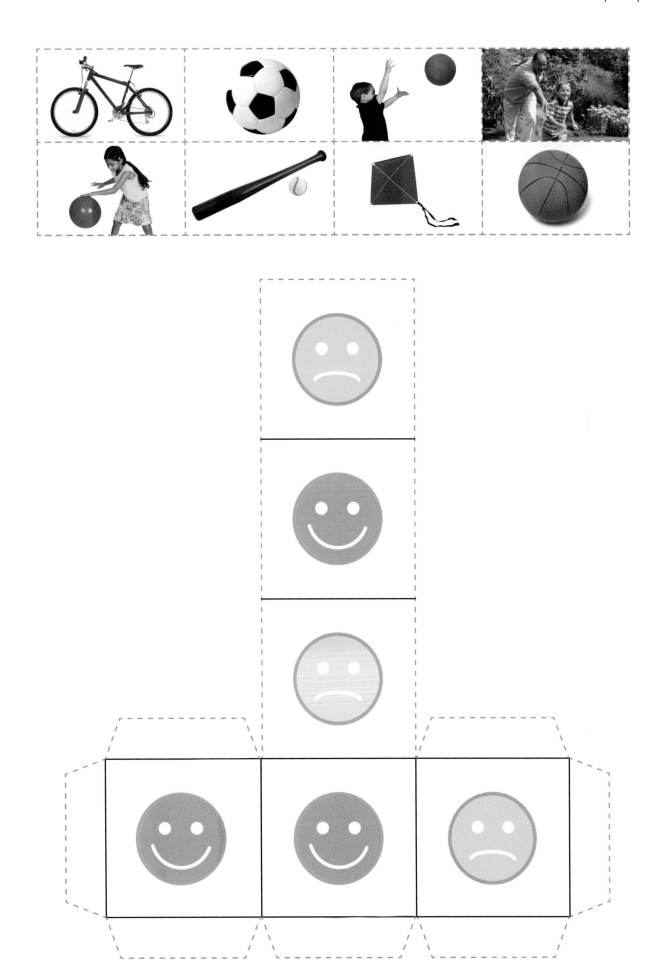

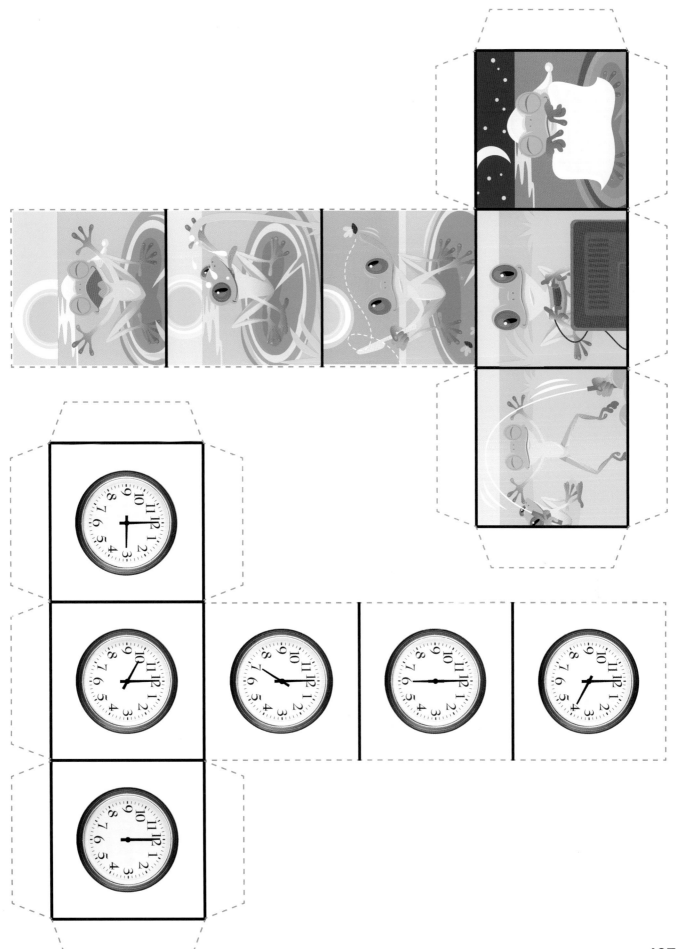

happy

sad

scared

laughing

bored

angry

yawning

smiling

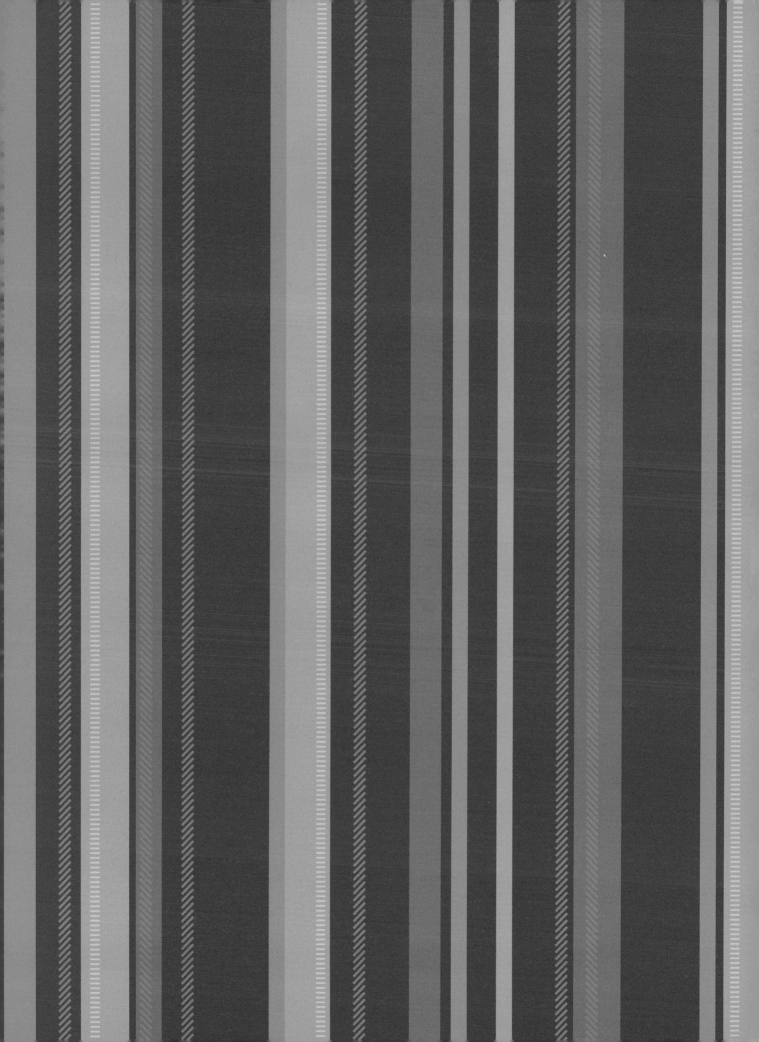